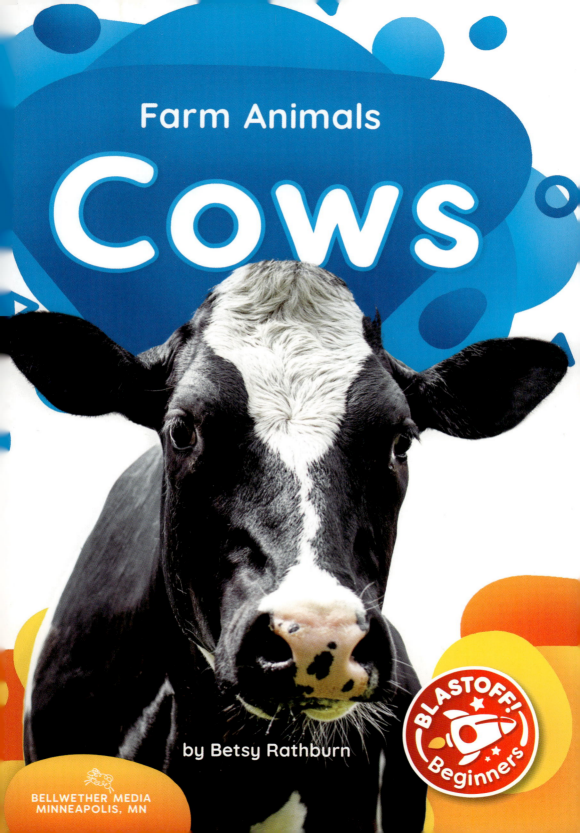

Blastoff! Beginners are developed by literacy experts and educators to meet the needs of early readers. These engaging informational texts support young children as they begin reading about their world. Through simple language and high frequency words paired with crisp, colorful photos, Blastoff! Beginners launch young readers into the universe of independent reading.

Sight Words in This Book

an	have	on
and	in	some
are	it	that
at	look	them
big	make	they
eat	many	

This edition first published in 2024 by Bellwether Media, Inc.

No part of this publication may be reproduced in whole or in part without written permission of the publisher. For information regarding permission, write to Bellwether Media, Inc., Attention: Permissions Department, 6012 Blue Circle Drive, Minnetonka, MN 55343.

Library of Congress Cataloging-in-Publication Data

Names: Rathburn, Betsy, author.
Title: Cows / by Betsy Rathburn.
Description: Minneapolis, MN : Bellwether Media, 2024. | Series: Blastoff! Beginners: Farm Animals | Includes bibliographical references and index. | Audience: Ages 4-7 | Audience: Grades K-1
Identifiers: LCCN 2023039744 (print) | LCCN 2023039745 (ebook) | ISBN 9798886877595 (library binding) | ISBN 9798886879476 (paperback) | ISBN 9798886878530 (ebook)
Subjects: LCSH: Cows--Juvenile literature.
Classification: LCC SF197.5 .R38 2024 (print) | LCC SF197.5 (ebook) | DDC 636.2--dc23/eng/20230831
LC record available at https://lccn.loc.gov/2023039744
LC ebook record available at https://lccn.loc.gov/2023039745

Text copyright © 2024 by Bellwether Media, Inc. BLASTOFF! BEGINNERS and associated logos are trademarks and/or registered trademarks of Bellwether Media, Inc.

Editor: Elizabeth Neuenfeldt   Designer: Laura Sowers

Printed in the United States of America, North Mankato, MN.

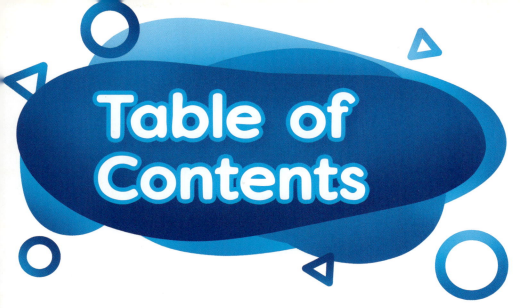

Table of Contents

A Field of Food	4
What Are Cows?	6
Life on the Farm	14
Cow Facts	22
Glossary	23
To Learn More	24
Index	24

A Field of Food

Look at that **pasture**. Those cows eat grass. Moo!

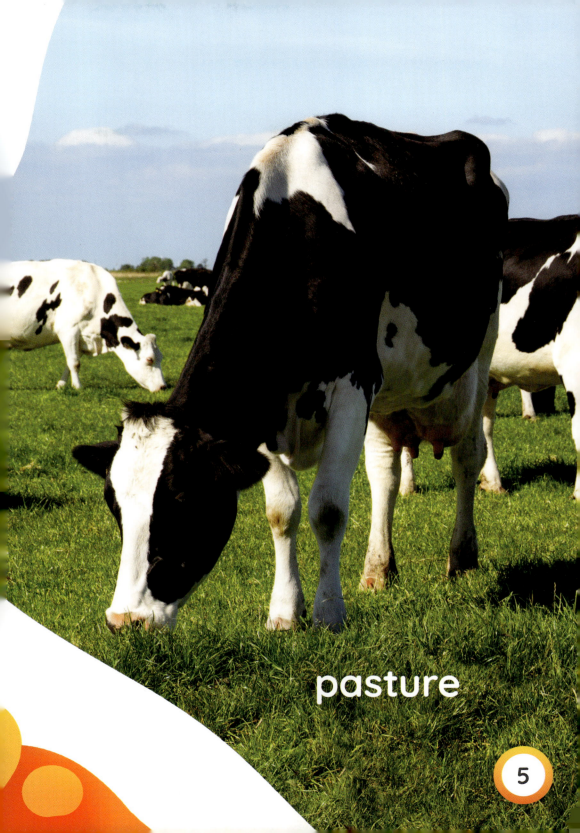
pasture

What Are Cows?

Cows are big animals. Many have short hair.

Cows have oval ears. Some cows have horns!

horn

Cows have **split hooves**. They have skinny tails.

split hooves

Females have an **udder**.
It holds milk.

udder

Life on the Farm

Cows live on farms. Farmers feed them hay.

Cows **graze** in pastures. They eat grass.

grazing

hay

grass

They rest in barns.
They stay cool.
They sleep.

barn

Female cows give milk.
It makes cheese and ice cream!

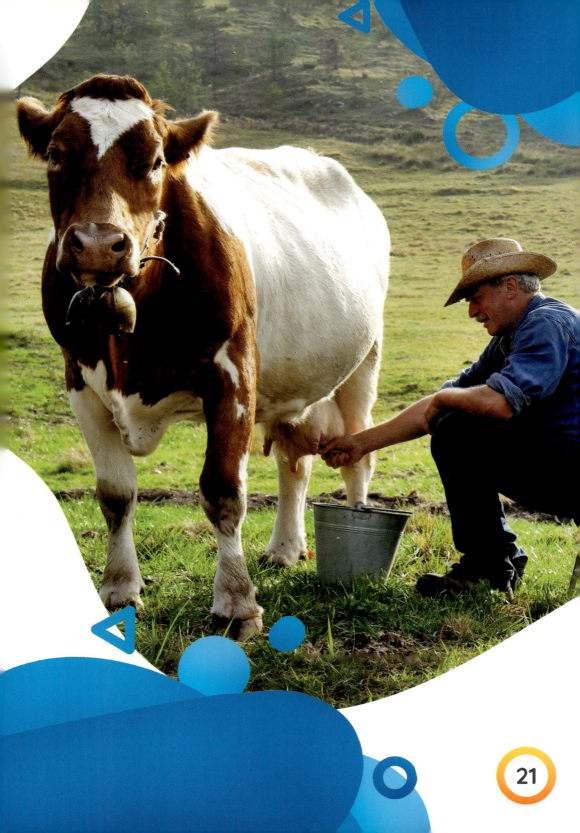

Cow Facts

Parts of a Cow

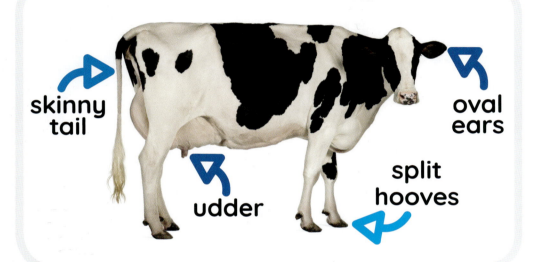

skinny tail

oval ears

udder

split hooves

Life on the Farm

graze

rest in barns

give milk

Glossary

graze

to eat grass and other plants

pasture

a field where animals graze

split hooves

hard foot coverings that have two parts

udder

a part of a female cow that holds milk

23

To Learn More

ON THE WEB

FACTSURFER

Factsurfer.com gives you a safe, fun way to find more information.

1. Go to www.factsurfer.com.

2. Enter "cows" into the search box and click 🔍.

3. Select your book cover to see a list of related content.

Index

barns, 18
cheese, 20
ears, 8
eat, 4, 16
farmers, 14, 15
farms, 14
females, 12, 20
grass, 4, 16, 17
graze, 16, 17

hair, 6
hay, 14, 15, 17
horns, 8
ice cream, 20
milk, 12, 20
pasture, 4, 5, 16
rest, 18
size, 6

sleep, 18
split hooves, 10
tails, 10, 11
udder, 12

The images in this book are reproduced through the courtesy of: M Kunz, cover; Eric Isselee, pp. 3, 22; VanderWolf Images, pp. 4-5; Catchlight Lens, p. 6; Clara Bastian, pp. 6-7; DnD-Production.com, p. 8; Leena Robinson, pp. 8-9; aodaodaodaod, p. 10; schnuddel, pp. 10-11; Commercial RAF, p. 12; Diane Kuhl, pp. 12-13; FXQuadro, pp. 14-15; smereka, pp. 16-17, 23 (graze, udders); SERASOOT, p. 17 (hay); Oleksiichik, p. 17 (grass); The Vine Studios, p. 18; Edwin Remsberg/ Alamy, pp. 18-19; Andrey_Kuzmin, p. 20; Kitreel, pp. 20-21; manuk R, p. 22 (graze in pasture); colnihko, p. 22 (rest in barns); Zacchio p. 22 (give milk); Patrick Jennings, p. 23 (pastures); Vladimir Konstantinov, p. 23 (split hooves).